The Magic of Roots and Stars
A Tale of Strength and Hope

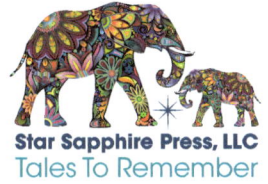

Debra Alessandra

Illustrated by Eleonore Hebal

The Magic of Roots and Stars
A Tale of Strength and Hope

Debra Alessandra
Illustrated by Eleonore Hebal

Copyright © 2015, Debra Alessandra, Star Sapphire Press, LLC

All rights are reserved.
No part of this document may be reproduced or transmitted in any form or by any means, electronic, mechanical, photocopying, recording, or otherwise, without prior written permission of the publisher.

ISBN: 978-0-9895213-1-4

Additional publishing & copyright information
Library of Congress information

Library of Congress Control Number: 2015918203

ISBN: 978-0-9895213-1-4

Copyright © 2015, Debra Alessandra, Star Sapphire Press, LLC

All rights are reserved.
No part of this document may be reproduced or transmitted in any form or by any means, electronic, mechanical, photocopying, recording, or otherwise, without prior written permission of the publisher.

Dedication

This story has two intentions. I wish to honor those who provide the special kind of support and strength children need. Additionally, I want to applaud the spirit of children who thrive and grow regardless of their circumstances.

For Mary, my friend and hero, who is raising her daughter's children: I have witnessed your strength, dedication, and grace for years. Adjust your halo Mary, you've earned your wings.

For Mary's three grandchildren: Somehow I know you'll 'get' the message of my story. I definitely wrote it with you in mind.

For my precious grandmother: Time and distance do not diminish the deep bond we share. Thank you for the special place you hold in my heart. The happiness I felt snuggling under your plum colored silk comforter every Saturday night of my childhood had way more impact on me than I realized at the time.

A Side Note of Interest

If you're curious why I chose a beech tree, let me explain. My grandmother, 'Baa', built the first house on her block in the town of Leonia, New Jersey. She was granted the honor of naming the street. She named it Beechwood Place.

Author's Note

The Magic of Roots and Stars: A Tale of Strength and Hope is an engaging story to uplift the growing number of children who are being raised by someone other than their parents. Many of these children become a little stronger and a lot more beautiful despite having experienced a difficult beginning. The transformative power of love helps them grow when they tap into the rare combination of resilience and fortitude in the face of an unexpected life.

The shimmering sunlight danced through the slender branches of the beech tree Amber called home. Clustered among the curly thin leaves all the flowers waited, their destinies unknown.

Mother's smooth sleek trunk stood tall and proud like a statue in a museum. She pulsed with life and swelled with the odor of newness.

The flowers clustered together in Mother's perfect mix of hardness and softness. They felt safe and protected. Even though the flowers looked the same, they were not. Each had their own name. In the slow cycle of life, every flower held the promise of possibility.

Days passed and the flowers turned into baby burs. They wondered, "What is happening to us?" None of them knew for certain. The warmth of the sun bathed the burs' tender coverings. The gentle rain drizzled on the short hairs of their backs.

Amber adored her home. She studied the sights and sounds of the woods. The moss and mushrooms, rocks and bugs entertained her. She squinted at the sun when it peeked above the ground and gazed at the moon when it rose high in the sky.

Creatures and critters filled her forest home. There were black bears, porcupines, raccoons, and pheasants. Red and gray squirrels joined them along with hedgehogs, foxes, and field mice.

Over time, the burs' bodies grew harder and thicker. Day and night, night and day the baby beechnuts talked among themselves, "Any minute now something important will happen," Violet said. "Should we be scared or excited?" Chloe whispered. "Hard to tell," Charlie answered. "Something tells me it will be wonderful though."

"Do you think we will know what to do and how to do it?" Griffin asked. "All in good time Griff," MacKenzie added. "We will figure it out when the time comes."

Spring and summer passed in the company of sugar maples and white oak trees. In pairs of two, the beechnuts waited as Mother turned from emerald green, to gold, to yellow, and to red. Then one day the waiting ended.

Like the pitter-patter of a soft rain, Amber listened as the beechnuts dropped from Mother's arms onto the woodland floor. The beechnuts hit the ground, rolled a few inches, and steadied themselves.

"It seems like a long way down!" Amber hollered. One of her brothers caught his breath and answered back, "Sure is," called Cooper. "If I had a spine, it would be tingling!" Even though they were on the woodland floor, they were still under the protective umbrella of their mother. Their chances for a new life seemed good.

Amber waited. Her sisters and brothers called to her, "Come on down, Amber. It's easy." She gripped tighter, "I don't want to let go, not yet."

Amber watched closely as Leigh shook herself off and straightened. "Hmmmm," she muttered. "Important work must be done and it must be done by me." Leigh continued, "Hey Amber, now I know what's next. If all goes well, I will be a tree myself someday."

Ready for a fresh start, Leigh began her work. She scrunched down into the dirt, sent out a tiny tendril, and gripped a small clump of soil. Next came the quiet born of waiting.

One night, the sky swirled inky black and dirty gray. Storm clouds grumbled and rolled through the forest. Mother's wet limbs swayed with the strong wind. More beechnuts blew to the ground. A chorus of "Whoa!" and "Oh my!" filled the air. Their voices faded as they scattered. Amber clung to her special spot.

"Hey guys. Where are you?" she called. She strained to catch an answer. Any answer. "Where can they be?" Amber puzzled. "Perhaps they're not too far away." In the deep silence, she made a big wish and said a little prayer, "I hope they survive."

The fierce winds forced Amber to loosen her grip. Up, up, and away she flew, then down she fell. She landed and rolled across the forest floor. "Where am I?" she quivered. "Where is everyone else?"

The sky rumbled and flashes of light set the ground aglow. From far away, Amber heard words of comfort. "Don't worry, Amber. You'll be okay." She tried to stop shaking. A slow inhale calmed her jittery breath. Courage stepped in to replace her fear.

All night she wriggled and squirmed and tried to settle in. Alone on the edge of the woods, she yelled, "Am I safe here?" No one answered.

When the first shafts of light broke the dawn, Amber trembled and thought, "I am so scared. I stand out like a big fat moon in the middle of a zillion stars."

The morning breeze hummed away the stillness. The rustle of insects and animals rooting in the underbrush chimed in. Small creatures scampered about in the shadows. In the distance, squawking birds broke into song.

Amber crouched down to hide. Large worries filled her tiny mind. "Maybe I am in danger. I can't defend myself. I wonder what's next." That same day she got her answer.

Yammerin' stammerin' Earl, the squirrel, stopped and stared. Earl wore a red coat. His bushy tail curled like a question mark. Amber studied his sharp teeth and the long nails on his feet. "Eww, he looks scary!" Their eyes met. Like a key in a lock, the combination of hungry and available sealed the deal.

Earl scooped her up with his claws and popped her in his mouth. He scurried across the ground toward his stack of treasure. When he arrived at his winter stash of pinecones, acorns, and fallen twigs, he placed Amber right on top. Then Earl stood upright on his two back legs, admired his work, and declared, "B.b.beautiful. B.b.better get more if I am going to survive." Off he ran.

"Well, at least you're not alone," said a voice. "Excuse me," Amber whispered to the other seeds and nuts. "Are we safe here?" But before anyone could answer, a large group of black birds startled them.

The noisy band of travelers perched to rest for a spell and hunt for food. Amber listened to their stream of whistles and songs. Rattles and whirrs filled the air. She wondered what all their sounds might mean.

And then she gasped, "Gosh. I may not know what they are saying, but I do know birds like to eat seeds and nuts!"

Amber was right. Starley, the starling, swished her short tail from side to side. Her wings laid long on her glossy body. Greens and purples glistened in a bluish base. Then Starley spread her wings and swooped down. She clamped tight around Amber's body and carried her away.

Amber twitched and twisted, quivered and jiggled. She fought hard to escape. As they glided through the air, Amber groaned, "This might be the end of me!"

All of the sudden, a clap of thunder scared Starley. Amber fell out of her beak. She plummeted down to the earth and became wedged between two rocks. Her heart pounded. Her mind raced. "Oh my," she sighed, "I am stuck and can hardly breathe."

She sensed other trees close by, but none of them were her Mother. Then she heard a calm and comforting voice. Her grandfather called her by name. "How will I stay warm Gramps?" Amber asked. "Just rest and wait." he answered.

The cold crept in around her and slowed her heart. Grandma dropped several leaves across the crack in the rock to keep Amber warm. Winter settled in. Amber rested and hoped she would survive.

When the marsh marigolds began to bloom, Amber's heartbeat quickened. She got to work. "I suppose this place will have to do." Her tendrils searched in the darkness. "Oh dear," she fretted, "I can't find any dirt."

Some days her work just seemed impossible, but Grandpa coached her and said, "You can make it, Darling." Grandma's words soothed her, "We are glad you are here."

Everyday Grandmother told her stories. She said, "Amber, a big tree lives within a small seed. A mighty oak grows from an acorn the size of a marble." Amber loved the soft sound of Grandma's voice. "Much greatness lies within you, my dear girl."

Amber relaxed and soaked in a few cool water droplets. Her body gained strength. What seemed impossible became possible. Amber gripped a clump of soil. She had found something to hold onto.

But, more hard work lay ahead. Everyday she stretched and strained. She was little, but she was brave. Even though she landed far from home, she fought hard to push upwards. Deep down she trusted her hard work would make her more beautiful. With Grandma's help she believed in the future. Grandpa gave her faith in things to come.

Amber's skinny tender shoot grew two small leaves. Then, two more appeared. She knew that size and strength mattered most. "This growing-up business takes a long time," she told Grandpa. "Yes, Amber," Grandpa replied. "You'll need years to grow. Remember, keep going no matter what." Grandpa and Grandma whispered, "We love you and we are here for you."

Amber wondered more than once, "What is the reason for this? Why can't I be with my mother? Did I do something wrong?" she asked Grandma. "No, my dear, you did nothing wrong," Grandma promised.

She thought, "The tree I am becoming is different from the others. I'm not sure I will ever figure out why." At last she decided, "Maybe no one will ever know why. I am not near Mother, but I am part of a Grandfamily."

Amber worked hard for her new life. Over time she grew taller and thicker. She peeked above her rock home and gazed at the beauty all around her. "My, it sure is lovely here."

Plenty of oaks and magnolias, cedars and pines stood on the far side of the lake. Most of them cheered her on. "You are special just the way you are. We're happy for you." A few trees teased her. They missed her greatness. Amber didn't let their words bother her. She stood firm and whispered to herself, "So what if I stand out? I don't mind." She remembered something Grandma often said, "No one can take your happiness away unless you let them."

In a universe full of wonder, Amber's struggle ended. She made a big decision – the biggest decision in her life. Strong and certain, she announced, "I've decided to be happy right where I am and exactly as I am."

When Grandma heard Amber's announcement her heart skipped a beat and then she said, "Now you can relax into your life." Grandpa added, "When we find and accept who we are meant to be, we honor ourselves and each other."

The more Amber grew the more remarkable she became. In the daytime, people came from around the world and marveled at her simple beauty. They took pictures of her and the interesting place she lived. Many shook their heads in wonder, "That sure is one determined tree." They squinted their eyes and scrunched their noses. "How can a tree grow out of a rock?"

Amber whispered her answer, "My grandparents are awesome, wonderful, amazing, remarkable, and incredible. They shared their hope and strength with me. Without their love, I might have given up." No one heard her explanation, but it didn't matter. Amber knew the truth. Somewhere deep inside, Amber had a bit of amazing in her too.

As night fell, Amber enjoyed the canopy of stars overhead. Teeny glistening lights flickered in the night sky. She adored the lake's silky carpet of blue. The still waters ran deep and held a special kind of mystery. Small waves lapped upon the shore like a soothing lullaby.

Amber inhaled the magic of the night air and claimed her place in the world. She understood she was a small part of a bigger picture, an incredible marvelous picture that included her.

Things for You to Think About

- The faces of families are changing.

- You are not alone.

- Millions of children are raised by someone other than their biological mother or father.

- You don't always get to choose where you live.

- Love comes in all shapes and sizes.

- People who love you take their role seriously.

- These people want to be a part of your life and stay near you.

- Often they have wonderful life experiences to share with you.

- They know your situation is unique and they do try to understand.

- Try to notice the good things they do, say, and offer.

- It may take a while to stop struggling and feel some peace about your situation.

- It's okay to feel angry or upset.

- If you talk about your situation, you will feel better.

- You did nothing wrong.

- Amber could have stayed in her struggle.

- Instead, she grew to feel happy where she landed.

- She came to understand she was just as important as any of the other things she saw.

- She could tell she was part of a bigger picture that included her.

- You are a piece in a larger puzzle which is not complete without you.

- Like Amber, you too are important and deserve to be happy.

Things for You to Think About

- Be extra kind to other children who do not live with their parents.

- It is a challenge for them.

- They may want to talk and feel a little scared at the same time.

- Be a good listener.

- They may compare and wish they had what you have.

- They may feel jealous or resentful.

- Be a friend by including them in your life.

- Let them talk about their situation without trying to convince them to feel differently.

- Let your friends know the situation is not their fault.

- Tell them who they live with doesn't matter to you

Facts about Beech Trees

- There are 11 different kinds of beech trees.

- Amber is an American Beech tree.

- Beech can grow from 65 - 110 feet tall.

- They can tolerate rigorous winter cold.

- A beech can survive over 400 years.

- Beech trees are popular for their beauty and the shade they provide.

- Their trunks are straight and tall like a temple column.

- The bark feels smooth and is light gray in color.

- Some people carve their names or dates in the bark.

- The wood of the beech tree can be used to make furniture, chairs, benches, stools, tables, bed frames, and coffee tables.

- Beech wood can be made into flooring.

- The roots of the beech tree are short, shallow, and slow-growing.

- The crown is dome shaped.

- Their leafy canopy lets little light through.

- The leaves are oval and have toothed edges.

- Usually the leaves are dark green, but they change color in the fall.

- These leaves start wide and get smaller and smaller and come to a point.

- The veins of the leaves are strong.

- Beech trees are called deciduous. This means they lose most of their leaves in winter.

- As the seasons change, the leaves turn colors.

- Some people like to use the leaves as a salad.

- In olden days, some people put the leaves in pillows instead of feathers.

- The leaves and bark can be used for dyeing fabric.

- Beech trees produce nuts known as beechnuts.

- The beechnuts begin as flowers.

- The male flowers are yellowish with red borders and appear in April.

- The female flowers are yellow, bristly, oval balls which appear in May.

- They bloom in the spring and are pollinated by the wind.

- The nuts that form inside the hard shell of the beechnut ripens in October.

- The nuts grow in pairs and hide in the spiny husk.

- The beech tree provides food for many animals.

- Many animals of the forest like to eat beechnuts as part of their diet.

- These animals include birds, squirrels, raccoons, pheasants, black bears, foxes, rabbits, porcupines, and wild turkeys.

- Long ago the nuts were used as food for pigs.

- The beechnuts taste a bit like a hazel nut or an almond.

- Humans can eat the beechnut and the oil it produces.

- The oil can be used for cooking or to make fuel for a lamp.

In Case You're Interested

Black Bears

Black bears usually live in forests. They spend the winter in their dens and live off the fat they have stored in their bodies during the summer and autumn. Most bears love to eat grass, herbs, and fruit. Sometimes, they eat fish. Their coats are shaggy with lots of layers to keep them warm. Mother bears care for their children for a long time.

Porcupines

The porcupine's body is covered with a mixture of long black and brown hairs and quills. The quills are used for protection. Some porcupines like to sit in trees. Trees give cambium and bark for their winter feeding. Porcupines cannot see well but they have a keen sense of smell. They shuffle and waddle along looking for grass, twigs, stems, and berries. Porcupines are creatures of the night who like to hide in caves, hollow logs, or in rock crevices. Baby porcupines are called "porcupettes".

Raccoons

Raccoons have bushy tails with black rings. You can tell a raccoon by the black mask across their eyes. Their front paws are nimble; almost like a person's fingers. Raccoons like to eat plants and animals. They shuffle when they walk. They are good climbers and strong swimmers. They are active at night and have excellent night vision.

Pheasants

Pheasants enjoy insects, vegetation, and the morning dew. They can fly, but most of the time they stay on the ground. Pheasants enjoy undisturbed grass. This is where they build their nests. The male pheasants are beautiful, colorful, and have long tail feathers. The females remain brown.

Red Squirrels

Squirrels will eat both plants and meat. They have bushy tails and pointed ears. With excellent eyesight, they can find food easily. They can jump 20 feet and run up to 20 miles an hour. When they are frightened, they run back and forth and in different directions to confuse their predators. Their front toes are sharp. The nests they build are called dreys. Their four front teeth never stop growing but get worn down when they eat nuts and tree bark.

Gray Squirrels

Gray squirrels are tree-dwelling squirrels. Like red squirrels, they build dreys (similar to bird's nests) made of twigs high in trees. The nests are about the size of a football. Squirrels are extremely intelligent. They are known to put on elaborate food burying displays to deceive onlookers. They make fake burials to trick potential thieves into thinking they have stored their food stock there. Then they bury the real stash elsewhere safely.

Hedgehogs

Hedgehogs like to stay in woodland areas. When they are frightened, they curl up into a spiny ball to protect themselves. They like to spend the day sleeping in a nest. They come out to explore at night. At this time, they like to root through hedges and other undergrowth to find their favorite foods, which includes mice, frogs, snakes, worms, insects, and snails. Sometimes you can hear them make a sound like a pig through their long snouts.

Foxes

A fox is a member of the dog family. They like to hide their food to eat later. They have many kinds of calls they use to talk to other foxes. Their hearing is very keen. A fox will eat almost anything but particularly like berries, insects, and small rodents. Did you know foxes have whiskers on their legs to help them find their way.

Field mice

There are over 30 species of mice. They have poor eyesight but great hearing and smell. Despite their small size, they can travel quickly. Their tails can grow as long as their bodies. They build burrows in the ground close to their food sources. These burrows are kept neat and tidy with separate areas for food, sleeping, and keeping waste. Field mice stay very hungry, eating between 15 and 20 times a day. Mice are quite intelligent.

Starlings

The starling has iridescent feathers on its head and chest. Their wings have a green hue. Their legs are pinkish red and their bills are pointed and yellow. They appear speckled because the tips of their feathers are speckled. They like to eat fruits, grubs, and small nuts. Starlings make lots of sounds and calls. Many people find them to be too noisy and rather annoying. Others love their beauty and only notice their friendly nature.

If Tree Could Speak

I stand so tall
Rooted in the ground
O' Creator I am yours

With loving arms
So full of life
O" Creator I am yours

I am rooted in awareness
Cultivated by your love
O' Creator I am yours

With a slowing light
You create a bridge
O' Creator I am yours

As you share your essence
I am transformed
O' Creator I am yours

I see the truth
Of how divine I am
O' Creator I am yours

-Cookie Von Linden

For more information visit my website at:

TheMagicofRootsandStars.com

The value of reviews is essential to the success of any book.

If you enjoyed this story, a comment or review on Amazon would be appreciated.

Thank you,

Debra Alessandra

To create a review, follow the instructions below:
1. Go to http://amazon.com
2. In the search block type The Magic of Roots and Stars
3. Double click on my book
4. On the right hand side click (# customer reviews)
5. Click to create your own review

About the Artist

Artist Eleonore Hebal has been drawing stars and trees since childhood. She is a student of literature, astrology, and herbalism, graduating from the University of Arizona in 2005, with degrees in Anthropology and Classical History. Eleonore resides in the Village of Amherst, WI, with her husband and two beautiful sons.

www.ingramcontent.com/pod-product-compliance
Lightning Source LLC
Chambersburg PA
CBHW041752040426
42446CB00001B/15